SEP 2018

LAKE VILLA DISTRICT LIBRARY

3 1981 00598 1133

How Plants Clean the Air
One Leaf at a Time

by Ellen Lawrence

Consultants:

Ann M. Dillner, PhD
IMPROVE Group, University of California, Davis

Kimberly Brenneman, PhD
National Institute for Early Education Research, Rutgers University
New Brunswick, New Jersey

New York, New York

Lake Villa District Library
Lake Villa, Illinois 60046
(847) 356-7711

Credits

Cover, © mycola/Shutterstock, © Garsya/Shutterstock, and © Vetapi/Shutterstock; 2, © Johan Larson/Shutterstock; 2–3, © Valentyn Volkov/Shutterstock; 3T, © Dashu/Shutterstock; 3R, © Lightspring/Shutterstock; 3B, © Dashu/Shutterstock; 4, © Frank Sommariva/imagebroker.net/Superstock and © Zadiraka Evgenii/Shutterstock; 4–5, © Stuart Monk/Shutterstock; 6, © Chungking/Shutterstock; 6–7, © Gary Whitton/Shutterstock; 8, © Sunny Forest/Shutterstock and © Joel Sartore/National Geographic Image Collection/Alamy; 9, © Power and Syred/Science Photo Library; 10T, © Dariush M/Shutterstock; 10B, © ArTDi101/Shutterstock; 11, © Leonello Calvetti/Shutterstock; 12T, © Becky Sheridan/Shutterstock; 12B, © Tetat Uthailert/Shutterstock, © Johan Larson/Shutterstock, © Lightspring/Shutterstock, and © Claudio Divizia/Shutterstock; 13, © Hurst Photo/Shutterstock; 14T, © Jahina Photography/Shutterstock; 14B, © muzsy/Shutterstock; 15, © yui/Shutterstock; 16T, © tmcphotos/Shutterstock; 16BL, © kuleczka/Shutterstock; 16BR, © Julia Zakharova/Shutterstock; 17, © Sergey Lavrentev/Shutterstock; 18, © Stephane Bidouze/Shutterstock; 19, © apiguide/Shutterstock; 19TR, © guentermanaus/Shutterstock; 20, © littleny/Shutterstock; 21, © Diane Cook and Len Jenshel/National Geographic Creative; 22, © Anna Sedneva/Shutterstock, © Pack/Shutterstock, © Winiki/Shutterstock, © DenisNata/Shutterstock, and © Ekaterina Garyuk; 23TL, © Gunnar Pippel/Shutterstock; 23TC, © GQ/Shutterstock; 23TR, © Matej Kastelic/Shutterstock; 23BL, © Vaclav Volrab/Shutterstock; 23BC, © ssuaphotos/Shutterstock; 23BR, © Power and Syred/Science Photo Library.

Publisher: Kenn Goin
Editorial Director: Adam Siegel
Creative Director: Spencer Brinker
Design: Emma Randall

Library of Congress Cataloging-in-Publication Data in process at time of publication (2015)
Library of Congress Control Number: 2014018026
ISBN-13: 978-1-62724-305-6

Copyright © 2015 Bearport Publishing Company, Inc. All rights reserved. No part of this publication may be reproduced in whole or in part, stored in any retrieval system, or transmitted in any form or by any means, electronic, mechanical, photocopying, recording, or otherwise, without written permission from the publisher.

For more information, write to Bearport Publishing Company, Inc., 45 West 21st Street, Suite 3B, New York, New York 10010. Printed in the United States of America.

10 9 8 7 6 5 4 3 2 1

Contents

A Very Helpful Tree............... 4
A Harmful Gas 6
Leaves Do the Cleaning.......... 8
Making Food 10
Making Oxygen 12
Every Plant Can Help............ 14
Cleaning the Air Indoors 16
Hooray for Rain Forests!........ 18
People Need Plants............... 20

Science Lab....................... 22
Science Words 23
Index.............................. 24
Read More......................... 24
Learn More Online................. 24
About the Author.................. 24

A Very Helpful Tree

In the center of a busy city, a little tree is growing.

It helps to brighten up the city street.

It is a home for city birds.

It gives people a shady place to rest.

The little tree is helpful in another important way, too.

It is helping clean up the **pollution** in the air made by cars, buses, and trucks.

How do you think a tree might help to clean pollution from the air?

Many sparrows make their homes in city trees.

Air is naturally made up of a balance of many different **gases**, including oxygen and **carbon dioxide**. Oxygen is needed by people and animals for breathing. When people and animals breathe out, they release carbon dioxide into the air.

A Harmful Gas

One of the gases that pollutes city air is carbon dioxide.

Harmful amounts of this invisible gas are produced when vehicles burn fuel in their engines.

Harmful amounts are also released into the air by power plants as they make electricity.

Fortunately, the little tree is able to remove some of this gas from the air.

cars producing carbon dioxide

pollution containing carbon dioxide

a power plant making electricity

Too much carbon dioxide in the air is harmful because the gas helps to trap the sun's heat on Earth. This is causing global warming, which is the slow and steady heating up of Earth's air and oceans.

Leaves Do the Cleaning

The tree removes carbon dioxide from the air using its leaves.

The gas enters the tree's leaves through tiny holes called **stomata**.

The stomata are on the underside of the leaves.

Once the gas is inside them, the leaves get to work.

They start using it in a way that will help the tree survive.

> What do you think the tree does with the gas?

leaves

The stomata on a leaf are so tiny that they cannot be seen with the eyes alone. It's only possible to see them using a **microscope**. A single hole is called a stoma.

stoma

In this picture, a powerful microscope has zoomed in on a leaf stoma. The stoma is about 5,000 times bigger here than in real life.

Making Food

The tree uses the carbon dioxide inside its leaves to make food!

To do this, the tree also needs water and energy from sunlight.

It takes in water from the soil using its roots.

From the roots, the water moves through the tree's trunk and branches to the leaves.

With the help of sunlight, the leaves turn the carbon dioxide and water into food.

The tree uses this sugary food for energy and to help it grow.

A tree's roots soak up rainwater from the ground.

A tree's leaves soak up sunlight.

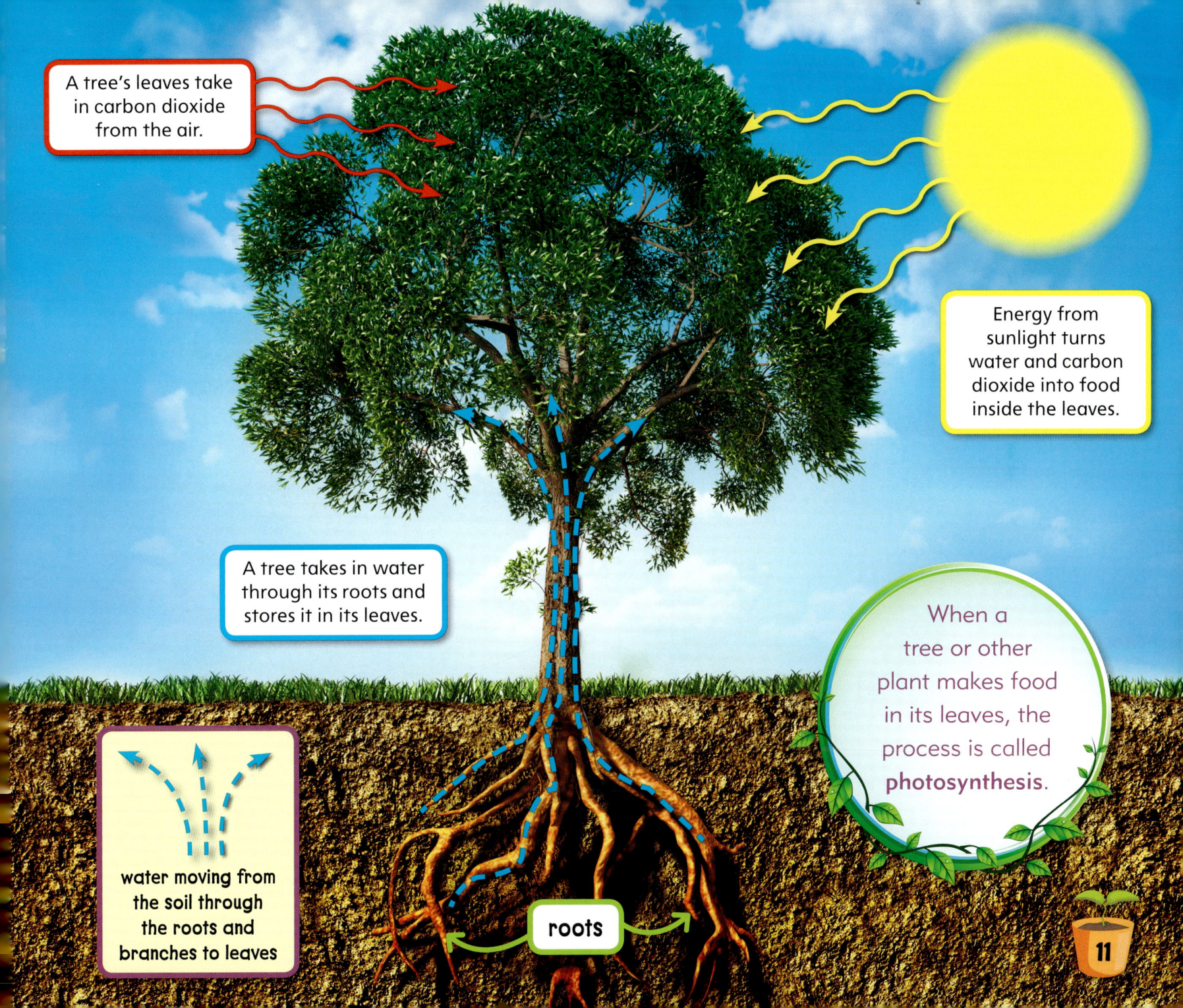

Making Oxygen

As the tree makes its food, it removes harmful carbon dioxide from the air.

It also does something else very important.

It makes oxygen inside its leaves.

The tree releases this gas into the air.

People and animals then breathe in this oxygen.

All animals need oxygen to breathe.

Go on a leaf hunt and try to find as many different sizes and shapes of leaves as you can. The leaves may look different, but they are all able to clean up the air!

Trees and other plants release oxygen into the air through the stomata in their leaves.

Every Plant Can Help

It's not only trees that can remove harmful gas from the air.

All plants, big or small, can do this.

Bushes in a park can do it.

Small, colorful plants in a windowbox can do it, too.

Even the grass on a soccer field is cleaning up the air and making oxygen.

How many places can you think of where you see plants? Make a list in a notebook.

Plants do a lot to remove carbon dioxide from the air. People can help, too, by making fewer car trips and using less electricity. This will cut down on the amount of carbon dioxide that goes into the air.

Cleaning the Air Indoors

Plants don't have to grow outdoors to help clean up air pollution.

Plants that live in houses, apartments, and offices can do this, too.

Their leaves remove carbon dioxide from the air.

Then they make oxygen and release it into the room.

The air inside buildings can become polluted by substances in paint and cleaning products. Machines, such as computers, also give off small amounts of pollution. The leaves of indoor plants help remove this pollution from the air, too.

Hooray for Rain Forests!

It's bad for Earth if there is too much carbon dioxide in the air.

So it's important that lots of plants grow on the planet.

That's why rain forests are such special places.

Billions of trees and other plants grow in these huge forests.

All these plants make oxygen and remove huge amounts of carbon dioxide from the air.

rain forest

Draw a poster that tells people why it's important to protect rain forests. One reason is that rain forest plants clean the air. Another is that the plants make oxygen. What other reasons can you think of?

(Some ideas that will help you are on page 24.)

a rain forest in Thailand

Unfortunately, large areas of rain forest are destroyed every day. Some people cut down the trees for wood or to make space for farms.

bare ground where rain forest trees once stood

People Need Plants

Plants help keep the air clean and safe to breathe.

So people need to protect forests.

Planting new trees, building parks, and growing plants in backyards are important steps, too.

Even taking care of a houseplant can help.

It's not possible to see that plants are helping us, but they are.

Every plant, big or small, is busy cleaning our air—one leaf at a time.

a young tree being planted in New York City

a rooftop garden on Chicago's City Hall

In cities, there is often little space for growing plants on the ground. It's possible, however, to grow grass and other plants on the rooftops of tall buildings. These plants can then help to clean up the pollution in the air.

Science Lab

Cleaning the Air

You can grow your own plants for cleaning the air.

As your plants make their food, they will help remove carbon dioxide.

They will also make oxygen for you to breathe.

If you grow some lettuce plants, you can even enjoy eating your plants' leaves!

lettuce plants

How to grow lettuce plants

Ask a grown-up to help you buy lettuce seeds online or from a garden center. Choose a type of lettuce that regrows its leaves once they have been picked.

1. Packages of seeds have directions telling you when and how to plant them. Plant your lettuce seeds in potting soil in flowerpots. You can also plant them in empty plastic containers—for example, large yogurt or ice cream cartons.

2. Place the containers in a sunny window. Put a dish underneath to catch extra water.

3. Water the seeds to keep the soil moist.

4. Soon tiny seedlings will appear. It will take several weeks, but the seedlings will grow into plants with big lettuce leaves that will clean the air.

empty plastic container

potting soil

flowerpot

seedlings

If you are using a recycled container, ask a grown-up to punch some holes in the bottom. This will allow water to drain through.

5. Remember to keep watering your lettuce plants.

Science Words

carbon dioxide (KAR-buhn dye-OK-side) an invisible gas in the air that plants use to make their food; plants take in carbon dioxide through their leaves

gases (GASS-iz) matter that floats in air and is neither a liquid nor a solid; most gases, such as carbon dioxide, are invisible

microscope (MYE-kruh-skohp) a tool or machine used to see things that are too small to see with the eyes alone

photosynthesis (foh-tuh-SIN-thuh-siss) the making of food by plants using water, carbon dioxide, and sunlight

pollution (puh-LOO-shuhn) materials, such as trash, chemicals, gases, and dust, that can damage the air, water, or soil

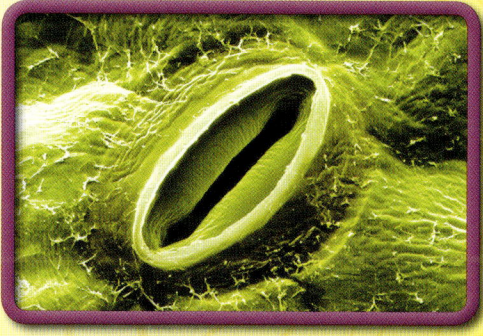

stomata (STOH-muh-tuh) tiny holes on the underside of a leaf that can be seen only with a microscope

Index

air 4–5, 6–7, 8, 11, 12–13, 14–15, 16, 18, 20–21, 22
breathing 5, 12, 20, 22
carbon dioxide 5, 6–7, 8, 10–11, 12, 15, 16, 18, 22

global warming 7
leaves 8–9, 10–11, 12–13, 16, 20
oxygen 5, 12–13, 14, 16, 18, 22
photosynthesis 11
pollution 4, 6–7, 16, 21

rain forests 18–19
stomata 8–9, 13
sunlight 10–11
trees 4, 6, 8, 10–11, 12–13, 14, 18–19, 20
water 10–11

Read More

Blackaby, Susan. *Catching Sunlight: A Book About Leaves.* North Mankato, MN: Picture Window Books (2003).

Edwards, Nicola. *Leaves (See How Plants Grow).* New York: Rosen (2008).

Lawrence, Ellen. *Global Warming (Green World Clean World).* New York: Bearport (2014).

Learn More Online

To learn more about how plants clean the air, visit
www.bearportpublishing.com/Plant-ology

About the Author

Ellen Lawrence lives in the United Kingdom. Her favorite books to write are those about nature and animals. In fact, the first book Ellen bought for herself, when she was six years old, was the story of a gorilla named Patty Cake that was born in New York's Central Park Zoo.

Answers

Page 18: Rain forests are home to millions of different kinds of animals, including many birds and insects. Many people also live in rain forests. In addition, many rain forest plants are used to make medicines.